THE SHOWER SCENE
from
HAMLET

THE SHOWER SCENE
from
HAMLET

POEMS

Daniel Lusk

Maple Tree Editions,
an imprint of Onion River Press
191 Bank Street
Burlington, Vermont USA

The Shower Scene from Hamlet
Poems
Copyright 2017 by Daniel Lusk

All rights reserved. No part of this book may be used or reproduced in any manner whatsoever without permission except in the case of brief quotations embodied in critical articles and reviews.

Book design: Lindsay Francescutti
Editor: Lin Stone
Cover art: "Between the Shadow," oil on wood, Patrick Carter
Author photo: Alison Redlich

ISBN: 978-0-9976458-2-8
Library of Congress: 2017912702

Publisher's Cataloging-in-Publication

Lusk, Daniel, author
The Shower Scene from Hamlet: poems / Daniel Lusk.
ISBN 978-0-9976458-2-8
LCCN 2017912702
LCSH Poetry, American. | BISAC POETRY / American / General
LCC PS3562.U7515 S4 2017 | DDC 811.54--dc23

Published by Maple Tree Editions, an imprint of Onion River Press
191 Bank Street, Burlington, Vermont 05401 USA

For Angela

and for them, the models.

Contents

1: The Artist's Model

Sleeping with the Cardiff Giant 3
Fireproof Women 5
Great Yellow Nothing 7
Damages 9
Call It Fondness 11
Pigalle Sketches 14
Orbits, Exile, and the Class Reunion 16
Reflections on "A Woman in Blue" 18
Here's Something Now 20
Ancestry 22
Monique Drying: Mixed Media 23
Points of Departure 25
The Guitar Lesson 26
Love, Erigone 28
House of the Hanged Man 30
When Night Falls 32
Blue 34
Mock Heaven 35
White Dream, Holy Moly 36
Nutmeg and Cloves 39
Even to the Next 40
Virtue, Even 42
Call It Gleaning 44

2: Footnotes to the Millennium

Going Up 49
Taking Responsibility for the Century 51
Exit Heroes 53
Poem on the Feast of the Epiphany 55
Sabbath Football 57
Pink Grenades 60
I Liked It There 62
The Shower Scene from Hamlet 64
Star-spangled Love 66
Friday Fish 67
Milo the Mule Face Boy: A Carol 70
Poem on the Feast Day of St. Paula the Bearded 73
Blood Oranges 75
The Butterfly Dream of Chuang-tzu 77
Only Flowers 79
Shooting Stanford White 81
Miss Smith and Mr. Ma 82
Lost Rudiments 83
A Map of the World 85
Crowd of Angels 87
Father William 89
About Desire 91
More Lies about the Presidency 92
Parts 94
The Jesus Pigeon 96

Acknowledgments

I am grateful to the editors of the following journals for first publishing poems that appear in this collection: *Georgia State University Review*, "Sleeping with the Cardiff Giant"; *Markings 30* (Scotland), "Fireproof Women"; *Massachusetts Review*, "Blood Oranges"; *New Letters*, "Call It Fondness," "Shooting Stanford White"; *Nimrod International Journal*, "Even to the Next," "I Liked It There," "Friday Fish"; *North American Review*, "Monique Drying: Mixed Media"; *North Dakota Quarterly*, "Ancestry," "The Jesus Pigeon," "Orbits, Exiles and the Class Reunion"; *Oberon*, "Call It Gleaning"; *Off the Coast*, "Pink Grenades"; *Prairie Schooner*, "Here's Something Now," "Lost Rudiments"; *Poetry*, "Crowd of Angels," "Pigalle Sketches," "Only Flowers"; *Southern Poetry Review*, "More Lies About the Presidency," "Milo the Mule Face Boy: A Carol"; *The Café Review*, "House of the Hanged Man," "Mock Heaven"; *The Chariton Review*, "Father William"; *The Comstock Review*, "Going Up," "Love, Erigone"; *The Laurel Review*, "White Dream, Holy Moly"; *The Salon*, "Blue," "Star-Spangled Love"; *The Southern Review*, "Taking Responsibility for the Century," "The Butterfly Dream of Chuang-tzu"; *Tribeca Poetry Review*, "Parts"; *Visions International*, "A Map of the World."

Readers will find gleanings from a dozen biographies and thousand years of the world's history, but I am especially grateful to Felipe Fernando-Arnesto's *Millennium: A History of the Last Thousand Years* (Scribner, 1995).

Thanks to publishers Michael DeSanto and Renée S. Reiner, who also published my first full-length collection, *Kissing the Ground: New & Selected Poems* (Onion River, 1999), for their unwavering support and encouragement for my work during our years of association and friendship. And editor Lin Stone, for her careful reading and unflinching insights during production of this and other books.

For their continuing respect and encouragement I am indebted to Association of Retired Faculty and Administration colleagues at the University of Vermont, in particular for a grant to support the completion of this poetry collection. To my dear friend, artist Patrick Carter, thanks for the use of his painting "Between the Shadow" for the book's cover.

1
The Artist's Model

*"...in the original version
she could be seen undressing."*

"Gesture and Flight" Ann Lauterbach

Sleeping with the Cardiff Giant

For hours the model in the drawing class
has published proof that gravity exceeds inertia.
Shadows of her skin are deepening.

Next time she removes her robe
her body hair grown coarser,
lines about her mouth
confirmed by charcoal on the newsprint
sliding into our portfolios.

She closes shop,
turns away toward privacy,
pulling on her clothes.

The poem the model writes in public solitude
should not surprise us. She might lie
for months upon a table in an attic studio.

Gradually longing is transformed
to intimacy, reinforced by every glance,
by cups of coffee shared beside his sketch of her
with those he loves.

Meanwhile she's reading lines, auditioning
for "Five Women Wearing the Same Dress,"
serving turkey sandwiches to tourists,
sleeping on the floor some nights
she weeps into the shoulder of a man
her yearning paraphrased by outcry
of the deaf cat down the hall.

(more)

Posing nude again while reading Proust
against a musty old gorilla salvaged
from the university zoology museum
dreaming as we stare across our easels
what irony, of lying with some wooden humbug
like the Cardiff Giant fashioned like a man and buried
to be dug up in a farmer's field. Who is not a hoax?

She feels that ancient goose who cranes toward her window
from across the courtyard as she puts out her light
might be the secret father of her only child
begotten of a sick old man as she bathed him well again.

Could be she's Lillian LaFrance on her Wall of Death
this studio a carnival and she a goggled star
motor car of her mind hurtling round and round
inside its roaring centrifuge.

She wants to believe the unlikely can happen:
miracles, outrage, passion,
this humdrum life may yet surprise
before a leak in the roof
destroys the image of herself she most wanted to believe,
sweet permanence of a single afternoon,
or this passing love she thought she saw in our eyes.

Fireproof Women

I am making toast for Egon Schiele
and his sister Gert, naked at Sotheby's.
Out in the yard the constabulary stand
with hands in their pockets. There was
the question whether firemen should be sent.
Someone calls to the artist and his model
to put on clothes and come out.
Either weapons are fired into the air
or windows in the apartment below are exploding.

Under the circumstances I throw myself out of bed
and kneel at the curtains.
A man and a woman limp away down the street.
There is the whine of argument, or of steam.
We hurry through hallways,
beating on doors with our shoes.

Imagine the artist before a judge,
who anoints himself with hemlock and egg whites,
and then, safe in his righteousness,
holds a drawing of a nude over a candle.
The courthouse, suddenly enflamed.

(more)

If I stand barefoot in a motel in Milwaukee,
police light exploding on the pillows
and the little Office sign outside,
there must be a woman beside me.
Schiele and his model also were called out of sleep
on behalf of townsfolk or maybe parents
miles away troubled by lewd thoughts.
Think of those early drawings, maybe Gertie,
burned by his syphilitic father.

A man and a woman and a constable
can be one unfortunate arrangement.
A charred mattress still smoking on the lawn.
All these men, whining in the shadows,
hoses at the ready.

Imagine painting a woman with raised skirt
wearing red stockings now worth two million.
There is this longing for fireproof women.

Great Yellow Nothing*

After the long slow rhythms of a measured life
suddenly a fire in the walls, sheet lightning
at midday, a bell sounding
as if from deep in the heart of the river.

How shall we measure danger?
Sister Podgorny, the morning after,
putting on clothes that reek of smoke, confusion
in her eyes and me saying a weak goodbye.

Before breakfast Paul Gauguin is sticking up posters
in the Paris railway stations and painting cows.
By late afternoon he is painting goats and flowers
and native women with baskets on their heads.

The far knoll is green with promise
and the model assumes the pose of a mummy
discovered in the northern Andes of Peru.
Her mouth is open. Either the wind blows
like breath on ashes, or an old desire comes and goes.
I will paint her the color of clay; her dreadlocks
her body daubed with dung and ash and mud.

I will ignore the fox at her shoulder
and the men who make noises that sound like poetry
the murmur of the devoted, that distant crowd.
I will ignore the silence of my loins,
put my head between her breasts, make owl noises,
feigning wisdom and happiness.

(more)

At the edge of the Great Yellow Nothing
Nebuchadnezzar is astonished and anxious
at the dream extruded on the palace wall.
Once I could read this handwriting.

Now the sheep moon, the eggshell moon
I cherished, is the banana peel moon,
the moon of barking dogs.

What have I forgotten?

*Sahara

Damages

1889. Opening night at the Moulin Rouge.
Flags, a wall of mirrors, gas footlights and chandeliers.
Flashes of flesh, froth of underclothes.
This tumult of the crowds—smoke-ravaged faces
of women; sweat-oiled faces of the men.

In Andre Gill's horrific painting
a man in a straitjacket.
That terrible imagining of my childhood
that I am the victim, wrongly pinioned here.

Where also is the dignity of John Dalton,
chemist, his pickled eye
in this jar on a shelf in Cambridge?

A man sits in the dry ditch
of a chronic hospital.
Does not know his leg is broken.
Does not acknowledge he is blind.
Being told again, one more time, he is
like us, learning of the bombing of Hiroshima;
every time we hear it, we are shocked.

Martin Luther believed the sun
orbited around the earth.
Name my religion after Ehrlich,
who vanquished diphtheria, sleeping sickness, syphilis.
Or Edison, who dispelled shouting in a crowded hall,
and dark below the cellar stairs.

(more)

When I was born, Enrico Fermi
received the Nobel Prize and in December '42
devised a miracle in squash courts of the University.
My Christmas gift when I was four was fission.
The bomb was for everybody.

The Moulin is filled on Sundays
with artificial flower makers and hoydens
escaping bourgeois homes to taste this damaged life.
These people are surely happy, though many
are infected and all are surely dead by now.
Shall I try to step over my shadow?

Call It Fondness
—after Marc Chagall

Why is this goatman in a tree beside his lover's
darkened window? Voices

an angel a chicken from the sky from the ground
who is not freed by laughter and a song?

Call it fondness, or rapture
that portion of the Book of Kells repeated
inadvertently by the scribe,
                      a mistake, no
a glimmer of eternity, inlay of gold in a broken stone
a butterfly joint where the old tree was weak
Nakashima's table is strong
how she who loved him loved that weaker part

the cock crows the bush burns the final *m* in the text
lay on its side, a blackbird, head
under its wing
                      another dream
where the beloved's children have been left out
pockets handbags hands eyes sag with disappointment

call it truth, call it godly, call it
beauty, her nakedness unbearable her face
upside down the man the goat the fish
are one with the flowering tree

(more)

as if a woman could rise from a bed of cilantro,
ascend, circumnavigate her own
desire clearly their bodies contradict
Standard & Poors and Barry Manilow and the sow
jumped over the moon

what bird barks from a pink hotel room
old news from the sidelines sport of kings
a woman with yellow parasol her smile
like a hare from a hat my love is asleep in the hay

in a heap, she's afloat, she's a sheep
property of another owner
red eye of the rose on the burning face
of the river

by the way what never worked
for us dog-bite kisses on a side street
flowers capsized on a stream of cloud light
a boatload of passion upstaged
by smell of purple basil
                        worked for Chagall
faces green
in apple leaf light never mind it was summer never mind

what these lovers' hands are doing
a man apparently dressed a passerby a woman
naked the tent of her coat against wild weather
against going further than this tree
erect between them, rooftops

in full flight.

A painting an affair of the moment, what is it
suspended from the pendulum of your hand, a bouquet
of lies we may tell ourselves
knowing failure of memory is really
failure of will leaving our hands

empty

this was it was never it
momentarily wind and rain blowing nowhere
soul pushed off course toward
an occasion you can wake from capsized

a name already dissolving
like salt on your lips
an accommodation something like

joy

Pigalle Sketches

Beardsley sits over a glass of milk
at one of the quieter cafes.

Public women flower in doorways
show their petal thighs banter
with bartenders passing barristers priests

a milling crowd of tourists lechers pimps
bureaucrats and pensioners remind
him of a day spent drawing at a nudist camp

a little girl appeared beside his easel
yellow hair ribbon a green stain
where she has worn a cross on her naked chest.
Her eyes amazed among the meat of bodies.

Someone at a nearby table sips a drink
remembrance of a lover crossing his mind
who was that woman stepping out of a blue sundress
smelling vaguely licorice and why
should he remember now—not only spice
that lingered in his beard, but shadows of her skin?
His eyes are closed. Dark circles

purple tulip on the Tarot card that shows the Fool.
Extravagant behavior is required. Take off your glove.
How might massaging of a muscle loosen memory
where someone struck in anger or in sorrow
fists against our chest or stroked us tenderly
until our bodies moaned with understanding?
This is medicine and free when we can find it.

Meanwhile, back at the Hotel Flagrante,
rising in the dark from sleep I wait a moment
for my head to clear before I put the lamplight on
to check the time. A voice from the direction
of my pillow, groan that might have been my voice
I thought, I've thrown my voice.
And was alarmed.

Surely a voice out of one's pillow is not interesting
as someone's voice out of a burning bush.

Nudes on the Rue Pigalle keep pairing off,
their hips their hands their foreheads touching.

Beardsley finds the eyes enchanting
darkly erotic winks shy smiles and leers
sloe eyes dark bruises heavy-lidded bedroom eyes
aloof eyes fathoms deep. Lynx hyenas crocodiles

along the street a tall woman moves in slo-mo
wearing only boots and a tiara, pink pig on a leash
before her, parting the wonderfully naked
human sea.

Beardsley, dreaming of Picasso
listens to his painful, labored breathing.

Orbits, Exile, and the Class Reunion

Whatever became of Maria Fitzherbert,
who lay with the regent and never was queen?
Passing her days on a train,
winding through villages of wooden houses
and painted churches, for love demands
more than a cascade of sunlight,
a scattering of half crowns on the rumpled sheets.

Ten years she wandered, a lost comet,
a vague idea, through the universe, fading.

I am on foot this first day of the year
and cars rushing by, all going somewhere
I have no interest in, except the ones hurrying
to meet a lover; those I have an interest in,
the ones excited, anticipating supper or surprise,
the one who suspects he will find her in the arms
of someone else—then he will have to decide
which of the two to kill, or his own sad ass.

Victorine Meurent, everyone loves her
as Manet's lucent "Olympia."
Yesterday in the Place Pigalle, she was that hag
playing guitar for her monkey to dance.

A priest and an artist attended her funeral mass.
Vestments and cloak at opposite ends of the wooden box,
air in the otherwise empty church painted
with smoke and residue of promises.
For his part the priest is young and meticulous,
folding the white napkin, wiping sanctity from the cup.

At the cemetery behind the Burger King
brass plates shine in puddles of rain
and a stiff wind blows the sanctified mutterings away.

I examine my eyes in the mirror while shaving
to see what enthusiasm is there today.

What do we want with any of these pictures?
Soul wants a dry place to curl in quiet times.
To remember itself and some unforgettable thing.

Gagarin is a small town in Russia.
Now it is orbiting the earth. What is that star?

Reflections on "A Woman in Blue"

Oskar Kokoshka puts down his pencil,
apologizes for chill in the room.

Mary Mersen lowers her shoulder,
unfolding her arms. Tips of her breasts
the texture and tint of her lips.
She stretches, arching her back.

She is not like those models turning to wax.
Not plain Lotte Mandl or the sad woman, Trudl,
making a fence of her arms
as if she were a field on the Russian Front
and the making of art, a battle.

Mary lowers her eyelids, draws the straps
of her shift and with barely a shrug covers herself.
She bends to put on her shoes, taking her time.

This was before the grisly war,
the stained bayonets of their boyfriends.
Every gesture was light and pure shadow;
every moment, a brush stroke
drew blood from the canvas.

Home again with his loathing and sickening dream,
Kokoshka must leave the young sisters
who played as he painted them,
consciousness now "a sea ringed by visions."

There are human acts that punish forever.
Unfit for models, the artist exiles himself
painting a doll, a handcrafted figure
free of regret and safe against recalling
in some "desperate hour
the delicate gifts of the female body."

Here's Something Now

Songbird by my window says:
"Sweet enough. Sweet enough.
                    Sweet, sweet, sweet."

The artist's model, a florist from town,
reclines on a broad window sill, facing the garden.
Old sycamores, a sleeping owl, a neighbor
in a hat, tending his yard.
                    From a distance,

say where deer lie in shadows of tulip trees,
she may seem a bowl of peaches,
a still life of terracotta, thatch and flowers.

How much secret beauty there is in the world.

Where is the traveler in the tale
who grew cold and sleepless on a stranger's couch,
his spirit, thin. Who went
barefoot and shaking to her bedroom door.

If this were fiction, he might enter and be warmed.
Might huddle next to her, her body kindling
his heart and his groin. Might reach for her
as if he cannot help himself.

In such circumstances giants, heroes
and others generously blessed may well be
overcome by sorrow. Might even ask
their hearts to stop beating for the sake of the story.

On the first night home from his journey,
a man looks at his wife on the other side of the bed.
She is weeping.

What is the question here, and
which of them will ask it?

Ancestry

What is sacred
but the air, the light, the rain?
Or what more powerful?
The gods have no manners.

The artist conjures with a burnt stick
and the body of this model emerges glowing
from the page. A few passes
under his sleeves, and he himself vanishes.

Listen to me:
Who lets his parrot speak for him,
or his dog to act in his place?
The woman is naked and I hold tightly
to my stick and eraser.

On the last night of the year, a mob
bearing torches approached a bridge,
fulfilling prophecy.
The drumming stopped but the songs
went on, the dancers invisible.

My grandfather Sissel put down his fiddle,
walked under a stone.

How is it great-grandmother left
the firelight of another century
to walk with me?
Brand-name religions, like dark seeds
poisoning the grain, deprived her people of speech.

In the country of ancestors, I travel unafraid.
It is my own house frightens me.

Monique Drying: Mixed Media

The young woman at the health club plucks
at her shirt, releasing clusters of passenger pigeons,
extinct since yesterday.
Sweat makes cloth stick to her body everywhere.
From her shoulders, ribs, sternum come these birds,
bright messages in forgotten languages.

She stands in a doorway, breathing deeply,
catching a draft, imperceptibly drying.
It is the turn of the century,
old artists working every corner of the room.

Degas studies her on the Stairmaster, flashing
knees and thighs, paints her arms glistening.
Giacometti loves her long and slender arm-swing,
stride elongated against the Nordic Track,
twists of hair twigged to her temples.
She skis onto a Tuileries lawn, pigeons clucking after.

From his velvet treadmill Sargent spies her
bending to the free weights,
the shadows of her shifting breasts.
Sweet dancer, sweet weight lifter, lifting easily,
lifting nothing.

Across the room Picasso eyes the mirror,
arcs a single stroke where Spandex isolates
two solid hemispheres. Birds fall to the carpet,
muttering. They feed on minutes.
It is a spoof of realism, the Age of Underwear.

(more)

Cassatt ignores the birds, surrounds the woman's
origami hands and hips, her hair with light.
Struck by their canvases, I imagine traceries
of sweat on her skin, residual
as missed opportunities in the fibers of her clothes.

As if their gazes crystallized and shrank for decades
like oil and lavender.

Finished with routine, Monique loosens her hair,
removes her clothes, places a towel by the tub.

Bored as usual with his models, Renoir stands aside
as she steps into the bath, splashes
water from a pitcher over her neck and shoulders
in a wanton, bright cascade.
Salt streams from her limbs.
Poets in shadow, tending the pigeons.

Points of Departure

Renoir is painting onions. Not faces
of the landlord's pretty children
or this bared onion of a child in mother's arms.

That famous boating crowd at the café—onions
among them. Onion women in a sunlit garden.
Onion girls who read with lowered eyes.

A blind onion crosses with her dog
against a wall of traffic.
He does not admit to loving her.
He disdains those socialist and revolutionary
onions favored by the wild Gauguin.

He writes from Naples that his models disgust him.
So these bearded onions—friends and poets.
His wife is an onion.

These are not water lilies; not sailboats
tacking near the Doges Palace, not the breasts of bathers.
They are aproned onions of kneeling washerwomen.

Sometime during the Bizet "Adagio,"
across the lawn from the musicians playing
from the cottage porch,
a woman lifts the hem of her Hawaiian shirt
and holds her nipple for her child, a gesture
once familiar everywhere. She smiles

and smiling in return Renoir says,
"Nobody knows anything about art..."

The Guitar Lesson
—*after a painting by Balthus*

How her body aches to play.
How this other yearns.

How the bridge of the pelvis
arches as upon a swollen river,
its taut, invisible strings.
Skin rages beneath the artist's brush.

How the o of the body
moans in the straining breast,
skids along rapacious fingers,
wrists and groin.

The painter cannot show
what we have never known.
Need not explain this troubling music,
this volcanic ventriloquism.

I am not myself, panting
to look on this wild intensity,
but some other who has overcome me
with his visceral soundlessness.

Say I was awakened
by the sound somewhere in the house
of hungry horseplay.
To sit up, put an ear to the wall,
and listen hard. Wanting only
what arpeggio, what glottal outcry comes.

These are not simple pleasures.
There are others in a different room,
telling their prayers.
They will say we should send away
this matter of the moaning.

I say let the moaning come.

Love, Erigone

"Tragedy begins with singing and dancing of goats."
—Aristotle

When painting the face is not enough,
or deep kissing titillated by a tongue stud.
And almost every mot downtown
sports an eyebrow, lip, or nipple ring, how

shall I divert young girls from hanging themselves
so they may ripen and grow wise and rich
and old? The world depends on them.

I will enter the deepest forest
and approach the one, primeval tree.
I will call them to climb, long-legged primates,
by hanging dolls and painted masks among its leaves.

When the tree is wild
with their weight and fingers and thighs,
its long arms madly waving faces at the wind,
I will urge them tie thick ropes to swing and play.

I will invite the oldest women to come—halt
and broken, white-haired, cranky, drunk.
I will ask them to pray, for nothing much is sure.
I will beg them not to howl or sing or spit,
or otherwise be frightening.
To call birds and bring the youngest animals.

Young girls know their lives
are tragic before anything.
Great danger lies in their own shadows.

They must be made to live until
they wake each morning, clapping their hands.

House of the Hanged Man
—*after a painting by Cezanne*

Think of the voice of viola da gamba.
Shadows and weeping.

From the secret graveside
we carried dried roses—yellow
of yarrow, ochre of rue.
We had wanted to pray, but could think
only of waste and indelible stain.

We hung them head down
inside the windows to signal defiance.
They remained until faded
beauty faded to monotony.
And the love—what lustrous colors,
what wild perfumes had been—
also had gone.

An intimate, animal sound,
wept into the shoulder
of a stranger. Who else could there be?
To recall without fear even
those moments
we could not believe our senses

even those that repulsed,
that we regret.
Shapes in the streets
that refuse to acknowledge us.

Sweet somnolence.
Weep shadows on window sills,
on doorsteps of the houses.
Cry our own shadows,
engraved upon them
when we were both alive.

When Night Falls
—after a painting by Paul Klee

birds and beasts disguised as shadows
in the sunlit trees, in corners of the window frames,
under idle eaves all day

come crashing down—cats dogs ploughshares hoes
hedge-clippers police batons and whistles, hockey sticks
tin soldiers driving gloves a pigskin soccer ball no

that's the moon, pretending to rise
from the roof of the mountains

All the lights in Edison's bedroom are on
he won't be wanting the brown cow's milk
he's gone

the souls of animals denied affection falling
chalk erasers lawn chairs crates of Hummel folk
snowplows and rubber chickens

what else? Snow domes
a bullet Andrew Jackson carried in his chest
dead weight of the man who sullied
his wife Rachel's honor, laughter
out of Annie Rogers' room upstairs in the Tenderloin
a moonlit gold train out of Deadwood

a blanket of blood and Slow
who earned the name of Sitting Bull

John Dennis' rage that his invention of stage thunder
has been stolen for Macbeth, the cause-effect
of artichokes and lechery, my heart's own cruelty
a thousand cases of Brownbastard wine
bestowing dusk and melancholy on the young.

Blue

Degas asks Mary Cassatt to pose for him,
tying the ribbons of her shoes.

Paul Gauguin leaves the stock exchange
and walks to the boat.

Chagall said at the time that everything
may change except the heart's research.

This painting of a woman is one thing
that changes us, this blue that makes us think
of shoulders we have known,
of shadows on her face in late afternoon,

for we imagine it was she whom we knew well
the artist painted in cold light of his studio.

Mock Heaven

A young woman bursts from the doors
of the library in Avignon, exclaiming
"Peecasso! Peecasso!"
After that,
you can't go anywhere in the world without regret.

Petrels fly through waves.
When I grow tired of flinging myself off swinging bridges
as if it were a measure of something,
I will, like penguins, abandon flight.

I'm sitting in another meeting when a new young mother
stretches abundantly. These affairs of the moment
remind me how lucky I have been,
diving for pearls in my own bed.

White Dream, Holy Moly

Snow keep us.
Snow keep my aboriginal heart.

Church parking lot on a summer day.
In a dream I admire my new yellow car,
purchased yesterday. The Lord,
dressed in a fine white suit, approaches
and holds out his hand for my keys.

To my surprise I hand them over
and watch, elated, as he zooms away in my new car,
disappearing up the tree-lined drive.

Snow keep us.

Madame Tussaud fashions wax masks
from the heads of guillotine victims.
This is an accounting dream.
Humpty Dumpty sits on the wall, looking anxious.
Why do we picture that egg as male?

Am I Mad Toulouse? Do I go out in red trousers
with a blue umbrella, a china dog under my arm?
Do I sleep with my walking stick, wanting
protection from swarms?

Or should we all go about like him, with an affable
keeper as if we were bears, the more exotic
for being led round by a boring saint?

Snow keep this heart.

In an upper story of the cottage next door,
mullioned panes thrown open, a fine woman
in a cream-colored blouse leans out
to water red geraniums
with a large blue watering can.
Her hair, sunny as her blouse,
gathered into a nest on her head.

Vuillard would have painted her
but I have only sentiment and a little love.

Such things to me are sufficiently holy.
When I was a child, listening in church
as my father sang, the Holy Spirit
was a great cobweb in the rose window
showing our Lord in despair at Gethsemane.
Father's hymn rattled the glass,
disturbing the least of the three holy Persons,
or a small spider working there.

Snow keep us, aboriginal.

In the asylum at Independence, where my father
vacationed and his father died of a broken heart,
I wanted there to be a little door
at the end of the garden, where an old lunatic
who stole hats would hide them
to use as chamber-pots.

I will imagine the secret element
of old Stradivari's enigmatic varnish
was pee.

(more)

I will carve a little man,
and fashion his coat from a bit of wool.
I will hide him with a stone rolled smooth by an ocean
under the roof on a beam in the attic.
I will be safe from my shadow, and the other dark.

Snow keep us. And the Lord, invisible.

Nutmeg and Cloves

Peeping Tom of Coventry was struck blind
for looking at Lady Godiva.

Late at night, I am standing in half-light,
drawing. This is the hour of sheep.

My model, Deirdre, does yoga poses.
She is the bridge; now the fish.
She is the downward-facing dog.
Breathing fire, she is able
not only to open, but to close.

In 1686 inhabitants of Magindanao
uprooted their nutmeg and clove trees
to make their land ugly to foreign predators.
How then would they love each other?

Truth be told, they prayed
and their nakedness was orchard
and beauty for them.

Tom said the lady swayed deliriously.

So we unhitch the ox from the carriage
and go forth, quixotic, wrists flashing,
saving our souls with whatever grace comes to us.

Who among us will not weep for being pardoned?

Even to the Next

Let us call her Madonna Earhart,
who taught us how life is a cloud
and easily lost.

This woman is the landscape of my drawing.
Here are twin sheep, and here
the foxes of my dreams, near a place
made holy before the Christians came.

When Amelia disappeared
into some paradise of the Pacific, I was conceived
and waiting under the hill to be born.
I must have known the languages of animals.
At my birth there came to the village
men and bears with lutes and drums.
No one but gypsies could see them.

It's quiet here now,
the huts of our childhood boarded up.

The image of this body on the page
is the thing eternal. The woman
will go back to her daily soap and water,
and I will grow older on toast and soup.

Once I loved living at the top of a tree.
From the top of my stairs eerie harmonies
of Bulgarian women make a jeweled canopy.
These lines and smudges on the page
are also on my soul.

This drawing lives on, even to the next
Millennium, borne in the chiaroscuro
of mountain slopes we will think we remember,
deep in snow foot-printed by foxes.

Here is the cave where I swam into the world
like Sancho Moluco the pepper merchant,
dressed all in velvet.

A true diviner does not stay to marry.
Earhart does not grow old in the suburbs.
The woman dresses herself and goes home.

Virtue, Even

There are two rules only:
  1) white comes forward;
  2) shadow recedes.

Taking time off, I watch the roof-scape
from the skylight of my apartment,
slopes and angles of the cavalry barns,
brick chimneys and metal cupolas,
my own cupola crowned with a star.

There is one proposal only: Breathe.

Bedrich Smetana, the Czech composer,
went deaf and was afflicted
with a high-pitched whistling in his ears.
The sky this early morning has the winter pallor
of the man being carried from the stadium.
I am three rows behind him.

Nine pigeons on the service wires—Patience,
Prudence, Cleanliness, Chastity,
Hope and comely Charity, Piety, Wisdom,
homely Fortitude—their fretful attentions
give away their names.

Where are the children of Jean-Jacques Rousseau,
taken to the foundling hospital?

We mean "savage" not "native," don't we.

We mean the ones who first crawled
out of the ground. Who learned
from the pines to stand upright.
And patience from the moon itself.
Who killed to eat.

All of us are facing Virtuosity, that intemperate clown,
who bobs and turns herself round and round
on the crossbar of the service pole
as if a pigeon might become, by subtle
movement of its feet, and indecipherable head-bobs,
as fascinating as a cardinal.
As if foolishness were itself one of the seven gifts
of the Holy Ghost; a virtue, even.

If I break a champagne glass against my skull
to impress Moustapha's woman friend,
will she think of me tomorrow,
seeing how her shadow conceals
all that may not be observed or spoken?

Heartbreak offers its own proposals.

I am selling this house and these virtuous pigeons.
The woman will have nothing to come back to.
I will not be able to come back either.

Call It Gleaning
—after a painting by Jean-François Millet

These women, bent from the waist
like hummocks in the stubble field.

An oboe player trying a little riff
in the empty hall after the audience is gone.

Call it gleaning, our gathering
of such straws, oddments we find
when we don't know what we seek.

Salmon and flamingoes wear
colors of the food they eat.

A boy of six hauls a bruised cornet
in a canvas shopping bag
down a frozen street to his lesson.

And cranes, whose yard-long trachea
loop behind the sternum
like the umbrels of trombones—
their haunting duets and *pas de deux*.

Three old women in the hotel
coffee shop, black from burka
to shoes, their haunting silhouettes.

And the spell in the hour after twilight,
when night like a fever
lets a man lost and afraid see veins
of skunk cabbage leaves and goldenseal

so his path becomes evident,
a beaten track among serrated Cinnamon
and Interrupted Ferns where in the day
no light fell and now no light released.

Some call it wishbone wisdom,
this divining by cornets and cranes,
ghost shapes of women,
by sticks and goose bones.

2
Footnotes to the Millennium

"...a love story...of all strange things, so late in the century, so late in the goddamned day."

London Fields, Martin Amis

Going Up

"Men first danced in one spot.
Then they began to move their legs."
—Rainer Maria Rilke

Rising from the seedling bed, Nurse Jenkins tells me
basil eases heartache. Yes,
and I'll get through the winter with a pail,
a dish and spoon.
Why can't love be simple?

Bathsheba Bowers gives up sex, retires
to a veranda in the country.   Visions
come - beasts and bulls in fields of heaven - she acquires
a following.   When painted Indians attack,
she takes to bed and prays that Providence
may intervene.   As in a movie, men bear her safely
to a boat, bed and all.

A meteor shower, thousands prepare for "going up,"
disrobing on the hilltops, clothing cows
in Ascension robes for children will want milk,
the journey being long to heaven.

Who did we think made those angel prints
in the snow? Why could we not have fallen on our backs
and let our bodies also find a fitting elevation?

(more)

Speaking of angels, Miriam Hargraves
doesn't like doing right-hand turns.
It's a balance thing and karmic.
One clubbed wing and the thought
of cartilage deposits on her rotator cuff,
an awkwardness in turning.

A century later I am waiting for Love
to walk out of the woods
playing an accordion, singing instructions
for the dance. In this world hands
must be told what to do, though they appear
made for grasping and letting go.

Taking Responsibility for the Century

A man stands in water, drinking.
What threatens, he will call wind.
What arouses his heart, he calls love.

He is aware of a world he creates
by connecting the dots:
a livestock water tank by a windmill in Iowa,
a box on the wall with a bell and a crank.
Life as epiphanies linked by non-sequiturs.
Ride a cock horse.

Montaigne was mayor of Bordeaux.
Mussolini was son of a smith.

I hear Benito, bellowing with passion,
leading his Blackshirts through the streets.
An association of malefactors.
But for a full moon, a lamp in the quilted sky,
it is the same tonight.

My father is running down the road,
racing with Lord Jesus, who holds
the state high school record in the dash.
I run with them, confused,
believing the war is over and the past secure.

(more)

Magritte sits at a desk, designing wallpaper.
He imagines anonymity and lampshades
and ubiquity. He dreams
of bowler hats and Charlie Chaplin.
He does not dream of that paperhanger, Hitler.

What does Mahler do on his summer vacation?
Soothe the tormented Wagner of his heart?
Cocktail glasses and pretty music
rain on burning Dresden.

It is hot water we are longing for on a winter night
when all of us are shouting in the streets.
We want coals on the hearth, oils and unguents,
and an end to barbarity forever.

Exit Heroes

1337. Edward I of England prohibits
on pain of death all sport but archery.
1340. His archers string their longbows.
The French fleet is shattered in a rain of arrows.

Steve Carlton pitches 27 winning games
for Philadelphia's losing team.
And why?

Devotion to purpose.

Last evening at the Contois,
Abdullah Ibrahim on piano.
On the ceiling overhead,
I see the gold reflection of the cymbals
and the shadow of the drummer's hands

like a puppeteer above the music
and moaning of the crowd.
A siren in the street swells, playing through,
and like a lover's old boyfriend,
briefly supercedes the song and fades.
The courthouse bell, almost in time.
We are not forbidden anything.

If the longbow killed off class advantage
in old human wars, jazz
loosened passion's underthings in newer ones.

(more)

The beginning of wisdom is doubt, said Montaigne,
whose brother was killed by a tennis ball.
Lefty and Abdullah, pray for us.
When you have played us glad, leave town.

Poem on the Feast of the Epiphany

So they came—wizard, alchemist
and khan, sure they would know it
when they saw it. Though the star

was perennial and a virgin birth
predictable as annual flowering
that heralds bitter olives.

As they were far from home,
the local gossip—that Lot's wife,
angry to be swaddled in his prurience,
was unwilling to go farther
from her home than pillars
of the Sodom saltworks—
was neither news nor evidence.

That the mud god,
who called down sacred rain when
naked maidens lay on pregnant fields,
was murdered by a ghost
would not be understood by science.

Being wise, did they seek evidence
the earth would tilt, the seas rise up
and ravage villages along the shores,

(more)

and thunderclouds consume the sky,
winds come unglued,
the firmament reverse its spin
if X being infinite equaled mortal Y?

Perhaps like Don Quixote
on his spavined nag, unhinged
they sought some proof
of calculations and imaginings

that onions mimic
the concentric universe,
that stars like cats and humans
are born blind and die the same

that mystery reveals itself
when at last they whisper
and implode.

That with every turning past the sun
time's measuring begins again,

that poems pulse
to the iambic of the heart

that purple dye and common
spices—when centuries have passed
—make kings of ordinary men.

Sabbath Football

"The setting seems in some way to be
at the heart of the matter."
—John Cheever, *Bullet Park*

Five hundred years ago, law forbade
women of Florence to wear buttons,
and in 1976 Jannene Swift of Los Angeles
married a 50-pound rock.
I wonder,
how do we re-ignite the torch of wonder?

The Cathedral of St. John the Divine
is one hundred yards from magnificent doors
to the goal-line at the altar.
The Saints are playing
and you've got a seat at the fifty-yard line.

The present moment is spectacular.
Not here, perhaps, but somewhere.
A double rainbow arches over all of northwest Iowa,
the placid wake of hail and thunderstorm.

What weather vanes! What hens and cocks
and copper pigs aloft upon the gleaming barns!
What glory for a child afraid of rain!

(more)

*   *   *

The stride of the ibis measures exactly a cubit.
Let's just say it's the length and breadth
of a cage roomy enough
for a laying hen
to live out the one prolific year
of her brief corporeal life
or a crate sufficient to hold legs and arms
and assorted parts of an average human
retrieved after a blast that awakened Oklahoma children
napping at kindergarten miles away.

Our thoughts at that instant, irrelevant now,
overcome the way the feeble lamp of a bicycle
is obliterated by lights of an oncoming autotrain.

Think of it, Human! We are a moment,
a candle in a sea of candles.

We go out; another takes our place, and money on it.
We might have drowned, bobbing for apples.
We might have heard applause before we died.

*   *   *

So what if we lost the art of making fire?
Deep in the Chocolate Mountains
where no trees have been in our lifetimes,
old ones sit watching small heaps of embers.
Children poke coyote bones at the coals,
making certain the watchers do not
close their eyes and lose the flame.

When did we stop holding hands with our twin,
the Divine? When did neighbors stop
calling us both by the same name?
In the course of progress,
we lose something at every turn.

What is it that I cannot find?

Eventually, even the mute will be required to speak.
Even the consultants and the liars.
Admit it: Leonardo was also gifted at the shot-put.

Those were the 60's, when underwear was optional.
When sorrow liberated us all.

Pink Grenades

Wailing of an infant skewers conversation,
skews the human universe.
Under the big top a bareback rider standing
on a farm horse, plodding round inside a ring,
loses her balance

falls into the path of a clanging midget firetruck.
Sirens bells hilarity trombones dismay a troupe
of clowns surround her is there
a doctor in the house?
A violinist?

What about the child? A memory.
A pink grenade in our viscera.

I am speaking of the small detonations of the past,
a mind unsprung hearing someone
in a back row crying. Isn't release
what we believed would save us?

Think of memory as that nylon fishing line
the oriole found to weave her nest.
Her crying like someone unhinged now she
has made her perfect bed and can't get out.

Aloft in fishnet and stars the aerialist
does not believe in her partner, her leap
toward his outstretched arms a martyrdom.
Darkness blooms, the spotlight fails to find her.
Now this whimper maybe inside us,
maybe a bird, a child lost on a train depot stair.

Creatures who live in flight rehearse
their lapses in their dreams. A net is a work apron.

Whose bird-brained idea was this,
a shortcut to happiness? This oriole's basket
more a trap than a net.

I want to believe scissors were invented
just for this small intervention, an answer
to simple prayers, and not to lead us
toward pornography and topless dancing.
Even so, the wheel gave rise to bank heist
getaways, adultery, the breakdown of the family.

Who says there is no salvation?
Tears were invented before the bomb.

I Liked It There

This moon's a basket.
I can't see what's in it.

I'm watching Marva's mother bind her breasts
after the birth of Kate to keep her milk
from dribbling out. Love is in it

pain, alternating like a see-saw,
in Marva's words, keeps life going on.
A letter in her strait-laced hand
in 1982 is telling how she landed
in a psychiatric hospital.

Meanwhile, a man in Ecuador
is weaving broadleaf grasses with his hands and feet,
his legs around his basket in the milky sky.

Of her time in safe-keeping Marva writes
"I liked it there."
What did I think I wanted,
confused and keeping quiet anyway,
snow melting, infant crying in the darkened room,
one love escaping out the window, new love
outside the door, bound tightly, leaking through.

Half-century ago I went by steam train
with my mother, changing in Chicago,
central station like a humid church.
A foreign country with dark citizens.
I watched a mother twice as large as mine, who nursed
her child. I still am watching.

What is this but longing our tongues transform into regret?
The marbled shell of a bird's egg, broken on the curb,
yolk still glistening.

The Shower Scene from Hamlet

A park near Prague.

Ophelia in a yellow hat,
one blue-gloved hand,
her bare hand with a cup of coffee,
having just arisen bright with sex
from Hamlet's bed,
observes two small birds courting,
their sweet vocabulary, sweet
intention of their song.

She has no names for them
so looks for traces in the brushwork
of their feathers, clues to forgery,
as if they were a stolen picture by Vermeer.

She has no names for trees here either,
lobed leaf like an oak, scarred bark
like plane or sycamore
(without the names she might be blind),
no mental files on these green flies either,
or this stream that murmurs
in a Cyrillic tongue.

Now I understand her role; she is
a fledgling actress in Shakespeare
summer stock (this was to be their honeymoon),
and now one of two women
bathing before us in a dream
that has no hint of plot or resolution.

One woman rises from the bath,
hair tangled, soapy water streaming to her waist.
Thighs and private fur glistening, she turns
her milky shoulders to the light.
She is not drowned and we
have not disdained her all these years.

Should I mention scents of fennel,
myrrh, familiar ribbons on her bed,
lace of lesser linens scattered on the floor?

Or that the other woman smiling naked
in the suds I think I recognize
by the flicker of a tattoo on her breast.
(Was I ever tangled like a kite,
caught in her branches?)
How to choose between them, Hamlet
will ask his dreaming self.

Which one might be true as any ghost
to his perfervid heart?

Star-spangled Love

Surely we are not meant to love so high.

Except feathers be fixed to the wing-bones of the shoulders
the body is a stone that never ceases falling.

How were our shadows like two angels,
        wrestling on a candle-lighted wall?
I hold my breath and watch the sequined circus women
        stretch to reach the bar, leap out and

feathered stones a trampoline of clouds

appear to fly.
If I stand too fast, it makes me dizzy.

Chekhov sits on the white apron of the Garden Theater
        pretending snow is falling everywhere.
Cherry trees emerge behind the scrim. A wagon passes.

Never for a moment could I imagine
        those spangled women drinking coffee at the
intermission stink like horses.

Did she coax me up her ladder? Did I follow, trembling,
        afraid for my poor life?

Friday Fish

My loves stand gazing upward at a rock bass
dangled from my scale; the fish's eyes
gazing toward a stream of clouds.
This is not Heaven. This is Market Day.
Along the cobbled landing, women
paying coin of sweat for coin of sea.

What is the price of longing?
I will wrap their catch in pages of the Post-Dispatch
admiring how this isle of women divides,
regroups and stares again. I keep an eye out
for a favorite. My illusion: that she cares for me.

    *   *   *

"...a chance sighting of a Dorset milkmaid"
led to Thomas Hardy's Tess.
At five she was freckled; at twenty-five, her skin
appeared to have been bathed in haddock's milk.

    *   *   *

An ocean away, the Queen on waking
claps her hands and servants enter with towels
and a basin of lavender water.
They will not see her lingering smile,
though the smell of sex is palpable.

(more)

Think of Marie Augustin, marquis who spent
fifty years in prison for whistling at Marie Antoinette.
Why else is she the Queen and men on their knees?
Should we not send her some wind,
or take off a glove in salute?

    *   *   *

Captain Smith puts down his knife,
releases a fish spine from his fist, and opens wide.
The peach-billed plover
keeping watch on his hat alights in his beard
and cleans his golden teeth.

Another port, His Honesty glitters through the town
on his encyclical and poor folk pray politely
he will be a saint. Each quarter hour
an age of man steps forward two steps, rings a bell,
and disappears in the shadow of Strasbourg Cathedral.

Who can remember the name of the girl
born to the Clements with only one eye?   Could see
a match struck at midnight in a steeple 50 miles away.
Who was her role model
if not a live volcano or a tower clock?

What child was not afraid of being seen by her?
Who did not turn his milk cow's head away
for fear of curdled milk?

* * *

Beethoven is a winter man. Sitting down
to his piano, he removes his gloves,
pours ice water over his head.
His thoughts, a blizzard.

* * *

Spring rain.
River valley invisible in mist.

Speak to me of equity, of ethics, poverty:
there is approximately one person
for every chicken in the world.
An average leghorn lays an egg a day.

Milo the Mule Face Boy: A Carol

Charlie Parkhurst was a woman, coroners discovered
        when that heroic stagecoach driver died.

Playing a sousaphone solo in the Presbyterian church,
        nobody ever broke wind quite so ethereal,
my nickel-plated lily horn provoking angels painted
        on the chancel ceiling to point and snicker.
This is district music competition, Iowa. I am full of air
        and close to God.

My judge stands up and turns to face the audience;
        she's naked. I am ruined for life.

Years later, Lizzie Collins will depose a dollar star and sit
        astride the tiptop of my Christmas tree.
She promises a gift of buttons
        stolen from the flies of customers.

        *   *   *

Cokey Roberts interviews the reclusive American Buffalo
        retired now to a farm without a TV
near the junction south of Nora Springs
        about disappointment and a breakdown in family values.
This nickel bison has avoided publicity, shunned the talk shows,
        but it's clearly time to speak.

Every year she joins a Living Nativity in the barn.
        No cameras allowed. At intervals
combined church choirs and Miss Phares's elementary
angels sing a homely carol. Dripless candles
        sway crazily when someone goes outside to pee.
There is a fire extinguisher in the manger
        disguised as the holy child.

       *   *   *

Does my principal mind being called a buffalo?
She says she's having dizzy spells, a facial tic,
        and tells a dream
of standing in a bark canoe
        at a five-way intersection of opinions.
An RV overtakes her from behind, and oompa,
        she's deposited unhurt but quite exposed
at a meeting of department chairs, bemused
but irrelevant as a white elephant at a yard sale.

Since she's been fooled before, Ms. Roberts is skeptical.
I'm playing Silent Night on my giant horn.

       *   *   *

The brass lamp in my study goes off and on
of its own accord. I read awhile,
        then think or write in the dark,
listening to my pencil drag
some memory or passion across the page.
        This humming at my shoulder
is the sound of time relentlessly passing.

(more)

Like mayflies, children of the streets live quickly,
        with any borrowed name or sign.
God blinks; an angel dies.

I lift my cup from the third shelf of the bookcase.
It's dark again. Kermiel, angel of Chance.

I have no business card, no permanent address.
I try to name a cause I would live and die for.
Playing sousaphone at funerals. Herding bison in Iowa.
                            Taking chances.
Are all the dwarves and bearded women under ground
      or in disguise?
Is almost anything perceived as normal these days?

Is this at all disquieting?

Poem on the Feast Day of St. Paula the Bearded

Unlike Rachel in the front row
of my class, who smiles
as if she wants me to believe
she cradles ripe fruit in her arms,

that fourth-century lovely had only
prayer to save her, only
God who made her comely to turn
the wastrel who followed her away.

Six centuries of heaven gone,
licentious Pope Silvester's
bedroom ceiling beams, cartooned
with crude, cavorting figures, show
all manner of bawdiness and sex.

Eight centuries on, some
old and wrinkled prostitutes
daubed their faces with crocodile dung
to improve their looks and fortunes
until sweat washed away the mask.

And finally a *pension* in Avignon
so small it made his darling cry.
And he, padding a dim hallway
in his socks to the naked w.c.,

(more)

he dreamed a girl who could levitate
so long as she clutched
the outstretched, crippled hand
of her brother, so long

as she kept talking and despite
the anguish of his face, torque
of his twisted body, she
like a feather in midair,

wind on every side.

The bearded lady in the circus
photograph has bewitching eyes.
Ermine-cheeked lover, may gods help us
if our fingers yearn toward
the peach-furred yoke of her quick derriere.

Patron saint of widows, wild
for assorted miracles.
If she will not mind the rose
in my teeth, my low birth and hirsute faith,
let her also be my saint.

Blood Oranges

"No one ever talks about the magma."
—heard on "Car Talk" (NPR)

1077. King Henry is doing penance in the snow
outside Pope Gregory's palace.
There is a question of desire.

If a fat man bears a chicken on his shoulder,
he will never starve.

Once you came to me, gorgeous in my dream;
your words were thrushes' feathers.
You removed your robe and rubbed yourself
against me, even the violet shadows
beneath your breasts. Even the damp curls.

Lady Jane was queen for nine days,
and I was king for ten. My subjects, these thighs
and glistening fingers, willingly traded
everything they owned.
You gave me two blood oranges, to remember this.

Who will not start up at the sound of the falcon's bells?
Will not shudder at the blow of a kiss on the cheek,
the model clothed, the artists naked at their easels.

(more)

And in the morning, a drop of dew
on leaves disguising the porch of your bed.
And in the morning, your clothes
where you cast them off, on the kitchen floor,
husk and evidence of what you offered.

Perhaps you will remind me
there is nothing like milk in these oranges,
and nothing in this bowl but soup.

Today all the answers are "yes."

The Butterfly Dream
of Chuang-tzu

In 1360 an ugly bodyguard
captured a hundred ships grounded in mud
and founded a dynasty.

No one offered him status
or encumbrance of a job.

What of the princess, washing towels in Constantinople?
She would be conqueror of the wild wood,
of land behind the wind.

Lord Fauntleroy confronts the burning bush.
We might suppose there will be good news
for the suffering and oppressed.

Where a cow with a moon-shaped mark lies down,
there is your city, and darkness surrounds you.
This was Chuang's dream.
Fling a stone among armed men,
they will kill each other.

For such prophesies in 1417 a powerless Pope
was pelted with offal, for the catapult had been invented.

(more)

Bohemund, a Norman hero of the First Crusade,
had lieutenants nail him into a coffin
with the stinking carcass of a cockerel
so enemies would think him dead.

At the turn of the Millennium
these palms are offered, this breast bared,
not in supplication but in sorrow.
Yet we suspect there is a luminous alternative.

Only Flowers

So, in the face of this silence,
this abundance,
this undertow of desire

I close my eyes and breathe,
an heir who leans to inhale
the final breath of the departing
to keep their knowledge in the world.

Oranges are often to be found here,
and we envision below her belly
the corner of a field where birds gather.

When the god laughed the fourth time
nothing happened.
The gasp of irony
entered Time in this disguise

and the god stood still,
like a man with his hand in his mouth,
to leave the joke unspoken,
saying it was nothing.

My face against your thighs, I thought you
patron saint of queens and of the poor,
the bread you carried in your apron
transformed by a miracle into flowers.

(more)

This is the fragrance that draws the root
into moist earth,
draws the child from its hammock and room
to light. It is this

soul follows across the world,
out of marvel and stupefaction.

Lying here, your smells lingering
on my body like disbelief,
shall I believe I am the king of Spain?
Do you remember light coming
through the blinds?

Come to think of it, we
are common people,
and we are blessed with noses.

Shooting Stanford White

900 years the mirror of the Pharos Lighthouse
guards Alexandria. Its eye upon enemy ships at sea,
they burst into flame.
Unlike the moon, mirror
of a vain dark beauty only the insane could see.

1610. Galileo confides that her indifferent light,
which set the toy boats of lovers' hearts on fire,
is stolen from the closet of the sun.

1611. Jan Cripes discovers the telescope's usefulness
for watching a woman undress for bed
on the other side of town.
The woman is Evelyn Nesbit in absinthe underwear,
just home from shooting Stanford White.

She peels her stockings off, silk ones he bought her.
She lays her pearl-handled pistol on the bed.

1613. Galileo confirms his suspicion the sun
has the world on a string. Men in bathrobes threaten him
with Evelyn Nesbit, and he takes it back.

Then that seer who understood the stars went blind.
Years have since confirmed blindfolds
as ecclesiastical attire.

Who will guard the children as they go
to fetch a pail of truth,
guided by a fable's pearl-handled light?
He must wear a paper hat
so the gods won't recognize him.

Miss Smith and Mr. Ma

In the missing pages of *Poema del Cid*
Miss Smith holds tryouts for the typing team
and 13 adolescents give up football for the test,
distracted by her knees.

In between Art Appreesh and English Lit
Julie Manet gets naked and seduces Chaucer,
at 15 awaiting ransom deep in France.

Cinderella's slipper was truly ermine and not glass,
an honest error in an aural time.
I'll now explain the felicitous ending
in which a chorus only nods or sometimes drowses,
stretching—languid, ample and preferably
unblemished—on a beach somewhere during Skip Day.

Sir Robert Clive gets no applause
for capturing all India
and Hercule Poirot is impotent to solve
the mystery of his author's vanishing.

Remember Mr. Ma begot a daughter by his concubine
and died of poison in his tea. Penalty
and loss of down.

We fumble at touch-typing, sigh to learn
about Clorinda, warrior princess, suckled by a tiger.
Could release her body like a spring
to throw the javelin.

We could see her at quarterback.
She fades to throw and pulses quicken.
Miss Smith just leaned toward the window.

Lost Rudiments
—for Nan Oslund Farady, 1942-1996

There was an ocean, everywhere.
There was a turtle 12 feet long.

No wonder stories linger of how the world began.
Like fossils in arroyos of our songs.

Outside the bitter river
live horse-footed men.
And infants, born clutching milky stones.

There sits a man with a lion beside him.
Giant fish swim through the trees.
I come there sometimes in my heart
to listen for your voice.

St. Joseph of Cupertino, the aerial saint—
you said he loved the Blessed Virgin, and so could fly,
easy as Beryl Markham in her white silk blouse.

The door of the temple is closed today,
for there is war.
I wonder if you see the tops of everything.
And whether you look back to see yourself, asleep.

Do you see how empty is this room
where I sit by a window under stars, awake.
The pond asleep, the endless mountains dark.

(more)

Five million years ago on a bright morning,
our kinfolk picked up pointed sticks and moved
across the savannah from a dry lake
toward a swift stream they had heard of.
Odor of sweat and dead fish filled their nostrils.
A dollar was worth nothing.
They had their sacred post, they were alive,
and that was surely something as long as it lasted.

They would not imagine, as you did,
David Hume at prayer.
Or Frollo the archdeacon falling from Notre Dame.
Or us, teaching metal to fly and plastics to sing
because we learned how.
Do you know our hearts, you who are sky-clad now?

A Map of the World

This infant footprint in the files
might show the road laid out for her.
Or chart her river and its influences.

The work of a child is to tend the wild grasses.
To learn the sunburnt smell of dragonflies.
To love deep spaces in the fern beds.
To separate petals of iris and rose.

Remember the wise one
was not just any mackerel peddler.
How might a woman balance
the light outside and the light within?

In a choir of a thousand voices, be silent.
In a crowd of shining faces, be a shadow.
On fasting day, turn from your mother's kiss.

Think how a long line of people and horses
wound across this land, past the edge of the trees,
past the line of mountains
toward the place they last saw buffalo.

Some days the soul flies out and the body with it,
trailing after,
the way a flamingo carries its feet in flight.

(more)

Work to know equally sun and shadow
and there will be plenty.
Pay attention where you go
and where you lie down.

It is said that madness is a foreign country
where one might gain favor as Aaron did
if one's walking stick bursts into flower.

Crowd of Angels

"Even without a giraffe there is nothing to hinder good government."
—Chinese emperor, 1415

Madwoman Mary Barnes drank warm milk
from a baby's bottle, for her mother's tit was dry.

And in the desert, Marco Polo said, even
by day you hear the demons chatter,
and more commonly the beat of drums.

Here is a Mongol painting of a crowd of angels.
Mouths ajar, they crow their acclaim for a giant cockerel.

It is spring in South Dakota. I hear the cock crow
and throw my wedding band to the torrential Sioux.
Did I expect an army of carp to surface
among the ice flows? I can't remember.
Another river, another drive-by divorce.

Then are these angels, or St. Volodomir's 800 girls?
One peccadillo and I'm set upon by a nomadic tribe
of lawyers, of whom as natives said of the Puritans:
"there is no joy in them, but only sorrow
and a dreadful stench. Their religion is not good."

(more)

Among this choir, the brewer Margery Kempe
saw visions of the holy family and wept
to hear them talk behind her back.
She soon was on the outs with God,
and all her beer went flat.

We'll leave the picture and take this plot.
Flute the bellows mender will play our cockerel.
Light will amplify the shadows of the audience
so there are giants in the Asian mist.
Shen Tu will draw the first giraffe, its tender horn.
Now, everyone, roar like lions.

Father William

> *"You are old, Father William, and your hair*
> *is so grey."*
> —Song from Lewis Carroll's *Alice*

Robert Schumann hears his wife has died.
The walls said so, his pen, he wrote the news himself.
There's proof—she hasn't written him in years.

Whelmed by the thousand voices of the all-state choir,
one tenor ceases singing just to hear.
Two hundred forty-nine reedy males call out
for longing. To lie among the altos,
heads upon their bellies,
to hear low tones and rustle of their breathing.

In time mad Schumann bore the tortures
of fabulary music in his head.
We are these reeds. These minor figures he envisioned
in some distant choir. Imagining our battiness
profound in some sadder and more serious time

where William Blake sits in his garden
naked with his wife as in a paradise,
conversing with the prophets.

(more)

Last evening, listening up and down
the neighborhood for an escaped love bird,
I heard two finches in a yellow pine.
They were not prophetic.

I see nothing romantic in either courage
or heartbreak.
Pope Gerbert, who failed arithmetic,
was also humbled by music.
Schumann cried all night when Schubert died.

About Desire

> *"That is why*
> *the man is talking, & as clearly as he can, to a horse.*
> *...he has chosen to confide in this gelding."*
> —Larry Levis, "Sensationalism"

Wear red, the fox said, and bring me offerings.
Let us assume Jacob, wrestling with an angel,
as the moment love occurs.
The ladder an instrument of desire.

Who will not long for time out,
when fire burning round the hedgerow
of his bed appears eternal, and the whole world,
even the green bush of his daily life, destroyed.

Devotion is unnecessary when our bodies,
beads and strings of our spines
and intertwining arches, fingers, hair are all there is.

We will be those gray-haired women
who owned but one eye and one tooth among them
but shared a cap to make themselves invisible.

I give you this ladder; you give me these ribs
and belly to lean on. This is not complicated.

The holy man Ninkai was a vegetarian
who ate small birds.
Hearing the engine of the stars, we tremble.

More Lies about the Presidency

Like it or not, there she was, the full moon,
a woman in New Orleans dancing on our table, her fluid body
just as Pope had said of faeries, "half-dissolved in light."

William Howard Taft has reached the apex
of his physical achievement, 350 pounds of president.
Had he chosen bigamy instead of fly fishing
with Teddy Roosevelt, he'd have married
a naked giant in the southern climes.

A rotund beauty; lives on fatty oils and fish.
Think of her dancing—
how earth is turning slowly with the moon.

Their sorrow shames all ordinary doorways, bathtubs,
beds and shoes. And hats, for certain of their progeny
reportedly were fledged with horns.

Truth is, before the dog pack of the media
savaged the cloak of privacy around the President,
rumor dogged old Harding's Florence
that she poisoned him. For any of a hundred reasons.
Mistresses—Nan Britton had a castle at the bottom
of a monument's reflecting pool. Their White House trysts
marked all across the District by a peal of bells.
She bore a changeling child, afraid of salt.
Folks during Prohibition said that Warren
had a mind as fertile as a parking lot.

Edith Bolling Galt, the second Mrs. Wilson,
grazed sheep on the White House lawn,
ran the country from the stricken Woodrow's sickroom
doorway while he was in the ether, all but dead.
Forged her own opinions and his signature.
Who knows what marvelous decrees she gave us?
Tax on sweat. Foreign aid to Brunei and Kuwait.
A tolerance for monarchy and slavery of a certain kind.

I was not there, so this is all conjectural.
Whose honest prayers are these, enveloping the city
every spring with cherry blossoms?

A gynecologist attended President McKinley
when he was shot. No lie.
Is this a mythic place or what?

Parts

> *"...there is a scale; a thumb is fixing the weight a little*
> —Gerald Stern, "Hot Dog"

Sweet dancer. Sweet weight lifter,
lifting easily, lifting nothing.

Now rise and tell your father's secret,
that one eye is blind on account
of a priest of the parish.

In 1014, Basil the Second of Byzantium
in victory blinded 14,000 Bulgars, except
one man in a hundred, left one-eyed
to lead the procession home.

How many causes
and how much courage for the lack.
I remember Tom the monster
of dim Crippled Children's hallways, his wires,
horrific scars, his boot and finger braces,

loomed beside me once and stabbed a wrist
against my arm so I would reach his wallet
with the high school photo of his handsome self
before the tractor rolled upon him.
The one eye now, rheumy, weeping.

I see you turn your head
and raise your arms for love of sunlight.

Five floors up, a man steps off a roof
onto a scaffold and lets himself down
to wash the windows. Plants inside
have multicolored leaves.
Far below a van rounds a corner.

Mine is also a minor part,
a walk-on in human history
like the tailed men of Sarawak.
You are Robin Leary as poor lost Ophelia,
naming herbs for the sake of someone
you might have loved.

The Jesus Pigeon

I dreamed of pigeons, thousands
in a flock, sweeping down
the streets of Burlington,
and one lone pigeon on a cottage roof
behind the university speaking softly
to the women there.

Who else will speak for me
and I remain accursed and dumb?
My heresy is practical.

I wear my clothing inside out,
and know the difference between
the image of a woman, nude
and someone's sister, lover, naked.
I burn the church's icons
in my stove for heat.

Last night while thawing breast milk
in the microwave, I heard the screaming
of another Mary from the mobile home
next door, and wished that I were deaf
to all religion, grief and pain.

I dream of shepherds
singing songs I do not hear.

And now these pigeons,
rising all in unison
for pity's sake.

Poetry by Daniel Lusk

The Shower Scene from Hamlet

The Vermeer Suite

KIN

Lake Studies: Meditations on Lake Champlain

The Inland Sea: Reflections (audiobook)

Kissing the Ground: New & Selected Poems

The Cow Wars

www.ingramcontent.com/pod-product-compliance
Lightning Source LLC
Chambersburg PA
CBHW020620300426
44113CB00007B/719